10.00

A Visit to the Nature Center

by Rosalyn Clark

BUMBA BOOKS™

LERNER PUBLICATIONS ◆ MINNEAPOLIS

D0992925

Note to Educators:

Throughout this book, you'll find critical thinking questions. These can be used to engage young readers in thinking critically about the topic and in using the text and photos to do so.

Lerner Publications Company
A division of Lerner Publishing Group, Inc.
241 First Avenue North
Minneapolis, MN 55401 USA

For reading levels and more information, look up this title at www.lernerbooks.com.

Library of Congress Cataloging-in-Publication Data

The Cataloging-in-Publication Data for *A Visit to the Nature Center* is on file at the Library of Congress.
ISBN 978-1-5124-3376-0 (lib. bdg.)
ISBN 978-1-5124-5564-9 (pbk.)
ISBN 978-1-5124-5046-0 (EB pdf)

Manufactured in the United States of America
1—CG—7/15/17

Expand learning beyond the printed book. Download free, complementary educational resources for this book from our website, www.lernerresource.com.

Table of
Contents

Time for a Field Trip

It is time for a field trip!

Today we are visiting a

nature center.

We meet a guide.

She will teach us

about nature.

She will show us

animals and plants.

The nature center has trails.

It is time for a hike!

There are many plants.

We see wildflowers.

Tall trees grow near the trail.

What other plants do you think you would see at a nature center?

We collect leaves.

The guide tells us which

trees they are from.

Look! There are deer tracks.

Deer live near the nature center.

The trail goes by a pond.

We catch bugs in the water.

We put them back after looking.

What other animals do you think live in or near the pond?

We stop and listen at the end of the hike.

We hear birds chirp.

We hear frogs croak.

What other animal sounds might you hear at the nature center?

Many plants and
animals can be found
at the nature center.
Would you like to visit
a nature center?

What to See at a Nature Center

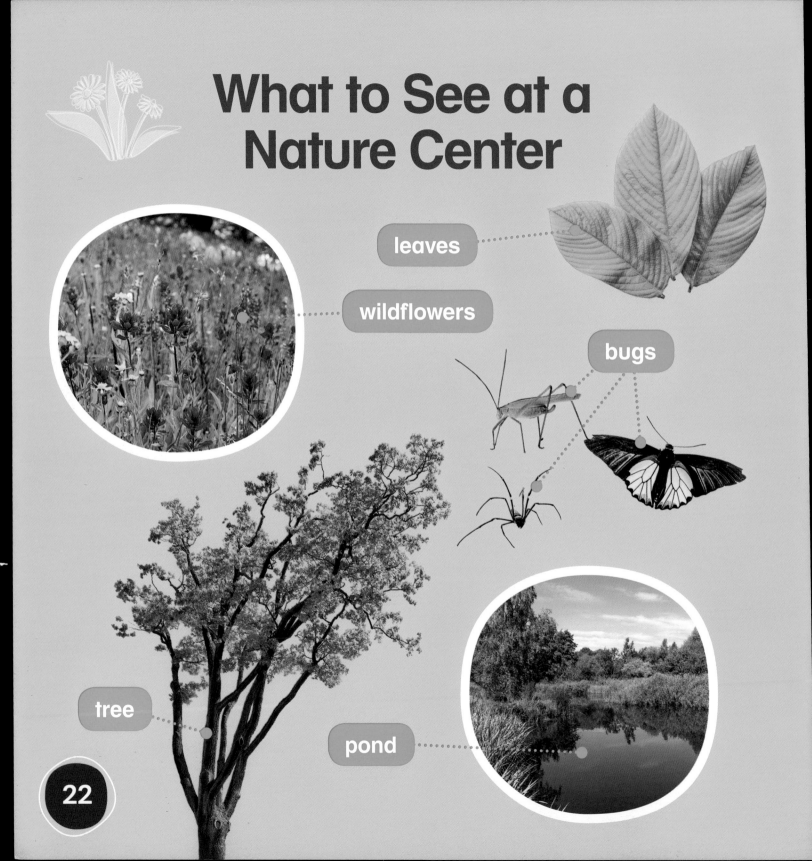

leaves

wildflowers

bugs

tree

pond

Picture Glossary

hike

a long walk in nature

nature

things in the world that are not made by humans, such as plants and animals

tracks

marks left on the ground by moving animals

wildflowers

flowers that grow without being planted by people

Read More

Nelson, Robin. *Deer.* Minneapolis: Lerner Publications, 2009.

Parker, Steve. *A Journey through Nature.* London: QEB Publishing, 2016.

Rustad, Martha E. H. *Do Trees Get Hungry? Noticing Plant and Animal Traits.* Minneapolis: Millbrook Press, 2016.

Index

Photo Credits